NO MORE CHAINS ON ME

"Freedom is the Oxygen of your Soul"

DOUGLAS G. LOEWEN

Freedom Planning Strategies

Freedom Planning Strategies exists to help families discover a life full of freedom so that they can live abundantly and in turn make a difference in other's lives around them.

Douglas G. Loewen
President, CEO & Freedom Fighter
#232, 3-11 Bellerose Drive
St Albert, Alberta, Canada T8N 5C9
Freedom@FreedomPS.ca
www.FreedomPS.ca

ISBN- 10: 1484133757
13: 978-1484133750

Disclaimer

I am hoping that everybody reading this book can be an independent thinker. This is not intended to be a book of research but rather a book of sharing experiences. I encourage you to learn from my experiences and then do your own research to decide whether or not you agree with my beliefs and convictions. The events in this book are all factual and not exaggerated; in fact they have even been toned down a little.

Introduction

My name is Doug Loewen. I grew up in central Alberta and have lived in this bedroom community my whole life. I have experienced my share of speed bumps and the subsequent scrapes and bruises (and the odd broken bone) due to some poor decisions and unfortunate circumstances. Many of you who are reading this book will be able to relate to the stories that I share and challenges that I have faced. But at the end of the day, I have been blessed to have another shot at marriage. I have been blessed to be able to maintain a very close relationship with my three biological children and have a bonus two more kids to be a part of what today is the Super 7.

Table of Contents

חופש הוא החמצן של הנשמה שלי

(Freedom is the Oxygen of your Soul)

Moshe Dayan

Pre Game

Have you ever been in a situation where you lacked oxygen; whether you were choking, needed the Heimlich maneuver, drowning or maybe you were winded and just gasping for air? Then you realized how much you took oxygen for granted.

I think of the time that I had to give a gentleman the Heimlich maneuver because he was choking on a piece of licorice. He didn't even say thank you. I think he was a little overwhelmed. He was minutes from death, he needed desperately to have a breath of oxygen in order to live another day.

Or the time that my older brother, in order to get me to submit, put me in the famous wrestler's sleeper hold and almost knocked me out. I could hardly breathe, I was gasping for air and desperately wanting to just have one more breath and get him off my back. This happened regularly; I appreciate your sympathy for this scarring.

Do you remember playing with the toy hand cuffs when you were young? It was so much fun to get cuffed and then to try and break free. But have you ever been arrested and handcuffed in the real ones? The feeling of having your hands behind your back, restricted, with no chance of breaking free is the epitome of bondage. Regardless of your possible innocence and the circumstances, you are at the mercy of the one with the key. It is a horrible feeling of having your rights denied and having your freedom restricted. It is extremely uncomfortable with the cuffs digging into your wrist, your arms twisted behind your back, your knees up to your chest in the small back seat of the police cruiser, your neck contorted due to the lack of head room. The bottom line is that it sucks the freedom right out of your sails.

For most of my life I have taken freedom for granted and now I realize that this freedom is the oxygen of my soul and is as essential as the oxygen in the air is to my lungs. I squandered my freedom by making decisions that put me into bondage. This caused me to gasp for air causing me to feel like I was drowning. I felt like I needed somebody to give me the Heimlich maneuver because I was gagging on our world's garbage. I wanted Big Brother to get off my back and let me out of the sleeper hold through which he had such a tight grip. I wanted to be released from the cuffs that were restricting my every move.

I see so many people who are themselves in situations where they lack freedom and so much of it is due to ignorance and laziness. This book is to help you understand how important it is for you to be free and how important it is for you to have this oxygen to breathe into your life. Oh how wonderful this freedom is!

My hope and goal is for you to get a taste of this freedom whether it is financially, socially, emotionally, intellectually or spiritually. This is what truly makes life worth living.

<u>Forward</u>

This book has been composed in a bit of a different way. I do my best thinking and dreaming when I go for my morning walks. At least six days a week I go for an 8 to 10 km walk and while I walk I also pray, I think, I listen to inspiring music. Often thoughts and words come to me that I know need to be written down in this book so I dictate them, email them to myself and copy and paste them into this book for you. It's over the last two years and 5,000 km of walking that many of these words have been put on paper to inspire you to live a life of freedom that I've been experiencing while enjoying God's wonderful creation.

So I invite you to join me on a journey like no other. This journey will cost you nothing but in a way it could also cost you everything. I invite you to open the pages of this book and join me on a walk that may be life changing if you open your heart and take an open and honest look at your life and listen to the life experiences that I will share with you. Approaching this book is similar to how you would approach a game of football or other sport. Before the game it is imperative that you do some stretching in order to be prepared. Then you need to put everything you've got into the game itself in order to play well. And then at the end it is important that you do a post game stretch and debrief in order to finish up strong.

I am having a challenge trying to decide on the appropriate level of transparency for a book. It is a bit intimidating to be so vulnerable to complete strangers. I have always been a risk taker so why stop here; I am going to do my best. After you have heard my story then I will give you an opportunity to reflect on your own life and do some introspection.

Once you desire and start seeking the truth then you will be heading in the right direction. This truth will set you free and this freedom is the only oxygen that can give breath to your soul. If this is where you are at then prepare yourself for what may be one of the best trips of your life. I hope you will benefit from all the mistakes that I have made in my life and how God has blessed me and my family through these lessons learned. He has transformed suffering into blessing and created beauty from something truly ugly.

What I am not going to be able to do is give a lot of application of how you can get to the same place in your life. Things are constantly changing and to put this into a book makes it too concrete and static. Since your circumstances are different from the next person's I want to be careful not to advise and then lead you in the wrong direction. This is a very personal journey that needs to be explored on an individual basis. I am not giving any advice or recommendations; I am just sharing my experiences and encouraging you to stretch your mind.

This book will address quite a bit about financial freedom because that's where most of you are going to be experiencing bondage and things are really going to hit home. But it can't stop there or I have just wasted a lot of time and trees because that is very temporary. I want to share with you a freedom on a much deeper level than just money. I want to open my front door and let you in and get vulnerable with you. I want to be an open book so you can really get a glimpse into my life and the amazing freedom that I am now living that goes way beyond my wallet.

In fact, I need to be real clear here before we get started. Money is very enticing to most. It has a lot of power and control over many. It has had a lot of control over most of my life. Until I was able to experience an incredible freedom that was unrelated to my finances, did I experience a true and beautiful freedom in my whole life. We need to be in control of our money instead of it having control over us. So let's not get it backwards. Yes we want to experience financial freedom but this can't be the engine on the train. If it is, then your train will run out of steam and you will not finish the race strong.

One of the strongest ways that I have experienced freedom that I will encourage you in is the freedom to be who you were made to be. Many lack the self confidence to live the life that they were meant to live. You were created with a purpose in mind and when you can fulfill this purpose, you are filled with a greater joy and strength.

This should all make more sense as we begin this walk together.

<u>My Story (the hard part first)</u>

1st Half

Sometimes the greatest part of learning is to hear someone else's story. It is preferable if we can learn from someone else's mistakes. But sometimes we need to learn by making our own – the school of hard knocks! I am going to try and paint for you a picture of some of the hard lessons I learned and the path that it has brought me down. I know right now that the words that I find will not do adequate justice to the despair that I felt during some of these lows but I will still try to open this door because I know that many of you will be able to relate on one level or another.

Throughout the book I will give you some ideas and thoughts that are completely outside of the box but I will also give you some "in the box" ideas that you can put to practice immediately while you figure out your comfort level of where you want to be in this delusional world.

But first allow me to share with you a little about George.

The Bonehead Kid

Chapter 1

George was a dreamer who loved to take risks; he loved to take things beyond what everyone else was doing. Whether this was some physical feat of strength or some awkward social scenario, he loved the reaction that he tended to get from those around him. His parents loved him and attempted to raise him to be a very responsible young man who loved everyone around. But what was different about George's background is that he was raised in a small kingdom which was ruled by a wonderful king and queen who also happened to be his dad and mom. He didn't know any other life other than this, which was one of great riches. If George needed something all he had to do was call and it was taken care of. He was totally free. He had no concept of slavery or bondage.

But there was a world outside of the kingdom walls that beckoned him and held something unfamiliar – something that almost everyone else was following and totally enamored with. There was a sense of discontentment and that made him very curious. There seemed to be so many promises being made that intrigued George. He could have so much. The dream was at his fingertips. So he decided to leave his parents and venture outside of the walls into this new life. It wasn't going to be easy at first but he was willing to try it, so off he went. There was so much that was foreign to him. There was so much opportunity to be a part of this new world. He could not figure out why his parents would have kept this abundant life from him. Now he was going to be able to do what everyone else was doing. He was going to finally feel like he was a part of the crowd and not an outcast.

The first thing he did was apply for citizenship in this new land of promise. He registered his NAME with the state so he could benefit from all the great things that they promised to offer. He received a special identification number that also enabled him to get a job which he had never needed before. George never realized how intricate it all was. He had so many applications to fill in. He registered to be a part of the state, he registered to get a job, he registered so he could pay his taxes, he registered so he could drive a vehicle, he registered just in case he ever needed to visit the doctor, he registered at the bank so he could use their services, he registered so he could travel and so on and so on. At the end of all this he felt that he had all his bases covered but his hand was quite cramped. Soon George was set; he could now do life the way that everyone was doing it. There was a part of him that didn't understand what he was doing but he saw everyone else doing it so he didn't question it. George thought that in order to achieve the dream he would need to follow what the people were doing because it sure seemed to be working for them. So everyday he went to work with the promise that one day he would be living the dream and reach his goal of financial freedom. Right from his first day, he had some hesitation about things but he decided not to question it since the people seemed so content and in tune with their whole system.

George worked 50-60 hours each week, then spent some time with friends socializing and had a bit of time at home to do a few odds and ends before turning in for the night and to start another dreamy day. This went on and on and became a recurring pattern until the weekend where he would spend his time buying things with all his hard earned money. He enjoyed splurging on things for his new place; he bought a new car and many other gadgets and doodads that he never even knew existed before. He would often be approached at a store by real smooth salesmen who offered to let him take his merchandise home without having to pay for it. He was constantly given a year or two before he even had to pay. This allowed him to buy so much more. He loved this opportunity and the endless experience of euphoria even if he didn't understand what he was doing. But as much as George enjoyed these things, there was still a feeling of being unsettled; that things weren't quite right.

One of the things that George could not get used to was how everyone around him was so motivated to earn these points that would give them the ability to get into more debt. It was like collecting some kind of slave rewards, quite the oxymoron. The nagging thought that was why anyone would want to be in debt, why would one want to be at the mercy of one of those bankers who seemed to have ulterior motives. It was like some kind of game to collect these points that would make it easier for someone to be a slave. It's about having a master and being their servant, owing them something even though not really understanding what they have offered in exchange. George grew up where all you needed was what you could produce. There was never any reason to be in debt to someone else. And if there was the slight chance that circumstances weren't favourable then someone would help out but there would never be any usury, this was strictly forbidden. And now he was living in a world where it seemed normal to be in debt and to serve this master called the bank and for those who had lots of these points accumulated due to good behavior had less usury and for the others, they were paying sometimes ridiculous amounts of interest each month.

The Truth Comes Out

Then George discovered something that caused him anxiety and sleepless nights. He learned that the reason why the banks were making so much money is because they never actually loaned anything in the first place. They received permission from the state to create the money from nothing. It was some kind of banking scheme that the government was manipulated into making legal a hundred years earlier through a bunch of complex laws and statutes. The banks would create more money anytime someone came in to borrow more and then they would charge interest until it was repaid. If the loan was paid off too early they would charge penalties. If a client missed a payment they would charge a penalty. And nobody seemed to understand this because there was always a lineup of people waiting to apply for more of these loans; they treated it like a privilege. In his father's kingdom this was fraudulent and punishable by a lengthy prison term. But these lawmakers somehow manipulated everyone into thinking that this was some sort of benefit. This was one more thing that he couldn't get used to and bothered him about this world that he chose to live in.

Then there was the SIN program. It was short for the State Indulgence Number. George had a difficult time trying to get over the acronym SIN which had such negative connotations. But yet he was expected to carry around his SIN ID and use it to redeem the different benefits that the state had offered. Rather than being responsible for one's own future the state would take responsibility for everyone's well being. It appeared as a program to benefit the people but under the surface George could see it for what it really was. He was beginning to see a pattern. It was a very manipulative way of having people voluntarily register into a program that would have them enter into these master-servant relationships, giving up control of their lives. He noticed that few ever questioned things. They just went about their lives accepting what the leaders brought forward into law. It seemed that every week the government had another 100 page document outlining more rules, laws and legislation that they voted into place. How was anyone supposed to understand let alone follow all these on a daily basis? It seemed far too complicated to understand …George wondered if this was intentional.

Often at work George would get into somewhat heated debates about all sorts of things with his co-workers. One of these was around the hundreds of taxes that everyone would pay without any understanding. He could not comprehend why people seemed so complacent with the amount of tax that they were paying. He would often question it and the integrity of the system. One of the factory workers tore a strip off of him because he said that it is their responsibility as citizens to pay their fair share of taxes, otherwise how would the roads, hospitals and schools be paid for. George thought that there was more to it than that; that there was some deeper level of corruption and cover up that the people couldn't see. He couldn't understand how a land so rich in resources could be so desperate for tax in order to take care of its people. There was some truth to uncover in order to open people's eyes.

George was so thankful that he was not born into the state. He had heard from his friends that when their children are born they can't be released from the hospital until they are also registered. The parents actually are forced to hand the control of their children over to the tyrant state by (voluntarily) applying for their citizenship or they will be held hostage at the hospital. As soon as they began this process they even changed the manner in which they would write someone's name. This was done so subtly so most would never question it yet it allowed the state to decipher between the slave (who they controlled) and the flesh and blood man (who was born free and nobody could control). Right from birth this seemed normal and once again is not questioned because nobody knows anything different, but to George it was blatantly obvious what was happening. It was one more thing causing anxiety and a gut ache.

Two Steps Forward, Three Steps Back

After a couple years of living in the state he found himself further behind from where he had initially started. Due to the fact that George had borrowed a lot of money to purchase a few things along the way he now had more debt than ever before. His income had not increased at the same rate that the price of goods and taxes was increasing. And now on top of all this he just received notice from his boss that due to cut backs he was being laid off as he was the most recent employee hired. He could no longer afford the place that he was staying in so he packed up his belongings and moved into a friend's place. Now he had no job, more debt than he knew how to handle; his toys were starting to rust and break, he still had taxes to pay the state, and a very uncomfortable couch that he called home. Lying awake at night wondering how he got to this point; he reminisced about the life that he once lived with his parents in the kingdom where there was none of this pain – a life of freedom where he was a slave to no man. But George quickly dismissed this as he didn't see it as an option to return to that life that he no longer deserved. He squandered the freedom that he was born with.

Very discouraged by feeling duped into this lifestyle that had caused endless headaches, George reflected on all the poor decisions that he had made and how he had become a slave to the state. It seemed almost impossible to find a way out. He decided that it was best to forget what life was like before and keep doing the same thing day after day, attempting to dig out of the deeper and deeper holes that he seemed to be digging. For 20 years he did the same thing day in and day out, never again questioning why, and totally forgetting his past life.

A New Friend

One day while George was walking home from work he noticed an older gentleman walking towards him. The old man called out his name which startled him. He didn't know how this old guy even knew who he was. He cautiously slowed down, yet stayed a safe distance away and asked him what he wanted and how he knew his name. The old man avoided the questions and just started talking like they had some history together. After an hour of hearing several stories George felt like he was chatting with a familiar old friend and that somehow these stories had some relevance to his pathetic life. All he could think of was how badly he wanted to be able to decipher what the old guy was saying but felt very overwhelmed and was starting to feel a migraine coming on. Knowing that this wasn't the end and there was more to learn he anticipated another meeting and that eventually the pieces of the puzzle would fall into place.

A month had gone by and George hadn't run into his old friend again. He was beginning to wonder if that was the end of it but somehow it felt like it was only the beginning. He knew that when he did run into him again he was going to make sure to have him fill in some of the blanks that had been left behind after their last conversation. The following day, just as he had hoped, he ran into the old man who he was still having such a difficult time trying to figure out. They embraced with a warm hug and then sat down and talked for a couple more hours. George shared with him some of his pain and struggles and was probed with more questions about his past. He hadn't shared this with anyone before. He began to talk about where he had come from, going back 20+ years. It had been quite a while since he had even thought about the drastic extremes in which he had lived.

He began to think of how much he missed that life being the child of a king and all the amazing benefits that it had. They far surpassed the benefits now being offered by his rulers. Giving himself a shake he realized that he was so far enslaved into this new life that his old life was unreachable so there was no point in reminiscing about it. But the old man wanted to hear more and kept asking questions about his parents and the kingdom that he had grown up in. Feeling good to talk about it yet so painful, it was forcing George to realize the many mistakes he had made, ones that seemed impossible to reverse. The old man said something that caused a chill in his spine. He asked if he thought his father would welcome him back into the kingdom if he ever had the courage to ask. Never having given this any thought, George never considered it an option. But it sure got him thinking. He missed his parents so much when he took the time to think about them. He missed his previous life in ways that were indescribable but he had a hard time remembering it because it was a lifetime ago. George sat silent for a few minutes thinking about what amazing people his parents were; they loved unconditionally, they gave sacrificially, and they led the kingdom in such a wise and discerning way especially when comparing them to the corrupt and idiotic rulers of this new land. He recalled how there was incredible freedom. Life was so simple. They were not bogged down by all these petty laws. It was all summed up by love, the golden rule: to love your neighbor as yourself. That's it. There was absolute justice and no corruption. There was no tax. The kingdom ran so efficiently and everyone benefited from the fruits of their labor. The king's role was to protect his people and not to interfere with people's lives. Therefore he didn't have all this inefficient bureaucracy that today George had unfortunately grown so accustomed to. This resulted in the people being allowed to keep all their earnings which resulted in more of a life full of abundance. It was a land with no crime. Nobody locked their cars or their houses because there was no worry, just absolute peace, that needs would be taken care of and there would be no scarcity. Everything that George has experienced in the last 20 years seems to be exactly opposite from what he grew up with. Now he lives in complete bondage; serves his debtors, obeys his masters, and is taxed to a ridiculous degree without any love, trust, or peace. All around are empty expressions on the faces of people without any hope for the future.

Like Vomit in Your Mouth

George had an ache in the pit of his stomach and an anxiety that he had never felt before, wondering why he would have ever left what was so perfect for such a mess. The ironic part that he just realized is how all of his friends and coworkers talk about the strength and freedom of the state. They seem so proud and patriotic. They really have no idea. They are really so far from being strong or free, they are the epitome of weakness and slavery. The country that he learned had once fought so hard for freedom is now a brilliantly designed labyrinth of laws and systems that has been designed to dupe the people to serve those in power who were elected as public servants. George hated this. He hated the decisions that he had made to be there. He hated that he had wasted over 20 years of his life and lost the abundance that was at his fingertips. He thought about the system that almost everyone jumped right into without questioning it. Those in power have gone to a lot of work to create an illusion of freedom. In order to do this they have had to change the definition of certain common words and make simple things very complicated. As a result the people just continue to be slaves without realizing it and have no idea of what true freedom actually is.

Is It Really You?

After all of this self examination the old man and now dear friend just looked at George with tears in his eyes and then the lights all went on. Finally George understood why he came into his life. George understood why he cared so much. George understood why he sought him out. George looked into his eyes and finally recognized him and his caring spirit. He was George's father, the King. He came looking for him. He had wanted George to come home so badly but knew he wasn't ready. Finally he had the realization of what he had been missing out on and how he couldn't go on any longer living this life of a lie. It was now time for him to live the freedom that he was born for and that his father wanted for him again. It was time to step outside of the corruption, fraud and deceit that George had been living in and the system that he had grown so accustomed to and had been a part of for way too long.

Why would George have voluntarily jumped into such a horrible world?

Why would George have allowed thieves and liars to govern him when he had the perfect King all along?

Why would he have wanted to live inside a fiction, a made up life when he could have instead continued to live a life of truth?

It was time to go home with his father and live in his kingdom again. For the first time in his life George realized that this freedom is the oxygen of his soul and he had been suffocating for the last two decades. So he breathed in a breath so deep and so familiar and let out a big long exhale that felt like it was cleansing him of all the weight that he was burdened with. He felt like he was turning a corner in his life that was a long time coming.

Coming out of the Closet

This is my story. I didn't really grow up in a kingdom and my parents weren't really a king and queen but on another level there are so many parallels. Lets jump in and discover how available this truth is and how once we discover it the freedom is right around the corner and can be inhaled as the oxygen of your soul as well.

My hope is that this book will help you start getting acquainted with this King. Unless you truly know the King, you can't begin to understand who you are as His child and without this you will be unable to realize all the benefits that come with this abundant life.

Nature or Nurture: Sometimes it doesn't Matter

Chapter 2

It seems that once we start down a road it can be difficult to turn back. This may sometimes be due to pride or ignorance. The fact is that throughout life we will make mistakes; some of these can be corrected but many have consequences that we will just need to live with the rest of our lives. When it comes to living a life of freedom most will never discover this truth due to all the distractions and illusions around us. But there are more and more people waking up and realizing that this 'matrix' is not real and that there is more out there. The masses sometimes view these people as radicals, conspirators, or doomsdayers. The life that they are living is just so different from what has been the norm so it comes across as a threat to life as we know it. Most prefer to just avoid it and keep living a comfortable life. I have chosen to take the other path. I believe that this one leads to the Promised Land. It may involve some ridicule and probably some lost friendships but once the truth is known there is no turning back. There are many bumps and obstacles along the way but the reward is worth it. Just be patient and learn what it means to take the journey and the impact on your life when you choose not to. Then you decide which road is right for your life. I know which one is right for mine.

I spent almost 8 years of my life working in a non profit organization called Young Life, having the opportunity to work with many wonderful people. Even after leaving this work, now a decade later, I still run into people and hear stories of the impact in kids' lives that I had. How very gratifying. I poured my life into others which had a cost. I made a lot of mistakes and I am still living with the resulting repercussions, ones that I will never be able to reverse. I made some choices that have created years of stress which at times I didn't know if I would be able to endure.

I was emotionally exhausted. I gave a lot to those around me. It's not like I worked crazy hours but when I was home my head was still preoccupied. And my family paid the price. They knew that they weren't my focus and that others were getting more of my attention and care than what they were getting. On top of that my salary was not quite enough to live on and we had a bit of an impulsive spending habit. So year after year we would spend more than we earned. This created debt and not just any debt, the high interest credit card debt that continually needed to be reconsolidated. So now on top of being emotionally exhausted I was also dealing with financial exhaustion which led to a deep emotional and spiritual exhaustion. Now I had even more to think about when I should have been with my family, not just in body but also in mind. After years of this, my marriage was a mess and so were my finances. This was definitely not the life that I signed up for. The next couple of years were the most painful years of my life. My wife had decided to leave me for someone else. I was struggling to build a new business. I was getting further behind every month with bills piling up. Suddenly now I was not a full time father to my kids, I was alone and I was a financial failure. I hit a point where I contemplated taking my life but I knew that this was not the path that my God had intended for me. This was almost the lowest I have ever been on the freedom scale (still a little more down to go in a later chapter) and the most depression that I had ever endured. But I eventually realized that I could not blame anyone else; it was a consequence of many poor decisions and some real bad timing. So this began my journey of discovering what true freedom is and how I could have it in my life and live abundantly the way that my Father, the King, had intended for me.

I knew that I would get married again one day. But it wasn't until I discovered and faced my pain and allowed myself to be healed that I would be ready for this commitment. I spent two years alone. I either worked or spent time with my kids. I was determined that I would not lose another minute with them.

Once I learned how to be content with my life and did not see a reflection of desperation in the mirror I knew that I was ready for 'the hunt'. It all happened rather quickly – 4 months to be precise. I met LJ in November 2006 and we were married on St Patty's day 2007. She found me online; you will have to wait for my next best seller – a romance. We blended our families and became the Super 7! Through some trials and learning how to blend a family we have experienced a roller coaster ride of challenges. But what an amazing blessing and memories that have been made.

The Super 7 in 2010

Show Me the Money

I want to share with you my financial journey because this has bled into every area of my life for many years. I never would have said that finances were my foundation but I found that they have influenced me in every other area: physical health, marriage, my relationship with my children, spiritually, emotionally and intellectually. So if we don't get a handle on financial freedom we may have a difficult time discovering meaningful freedom in any of these other areas.

32

The worst day of my life. What do you think? −N. Dynamite

One of the biggest mistakes that I have made that has caused a mountain of pain is that I began to apply some of the principles in this book before I really truly understood them and the implications of living them out. And I also did not truly consider the impact that these decisions would have on my family. This was one of the most selfish decisions that I have ever made and it has taken me years to find resolve. It was an extremely stressful time in my life so I took a desperate approach to try and fix some things and it landed me in a lot of trouble. It's not that what I was doing was incorrect; it's more that I didn't know how to approach it best and defend my position of truth that I was standing on. (If I was single, I may still be in fight mode today.)

As a result of almost 10 years of personal learning and some excruciatingly painful sudden financial stress I made a decision to very quickly start exercising my new knowledge. Because of my impulsive nature and general deficiency to detail I started this journey unprepared and a little too abruptly.

So I began exercising my freedoms when it came to my relationship with my mortgage lender, a few different government agencies and the law. I felt convicted of the truth and that it was time to start taking action in these areas.

It all started on July 27. My mortgage company was taking me to court and trying to foreclose on our acreage. I had served them with documentation asking them for proof that they were actually the party of interest in this debt and not just the service provider. I also was seeking proof of what was actually lent in the first place. As a result of all the research that I had done I was certain that the debt that I was obligated to pay them had been securitized to a third party and was no longer theirs to collect on. I also discovered that they only created credit with my authorization and did not actually loan me anything at all. (Go to www.FreedomPS.ca/category/debt-and-taxes to watch a 13 year old explain it) This is FRAUD (legalized by our government). After several months of them ignoring my requests for proof and me no longer paying the mortgage I was standing in court hoping that the judge would act on the truth. I was in for a big shock! The judge was on the bank's side. He ignored all of my requests, referred to my statements as 'gobblygook' and pushed my case through. The bank's lawyer just shook his head at me and the judge mocked me and had a good laugh at my expense. I was beaten by the system as well as beat up and bruised by a ruthless judge and lawyer. I was disappointed but at the same time prepared for the possibility that we would leave our home in order to finally sever the relationship with the lender.

While I was driving home to meet with the realtor who was going to list our home, I got a call from my office. Apparently someone was waiting at my office to see me. I swung by there to find two CRA investigators waiting for me with badges and briefcases. After 20 minutes of being hammered with questions regarding an educational organization that I was affiliated with years back, they left with many unanswered questions. I knew that this attack was not finished.

I got home only to find the realtor already there waiting to list our home. A few minutes later the doorbell rang and I was totally dumbfounded to find that the Sheriff was there to seize my car due to another unrelated issue (unpaid and disputed spousal support. I convinced her to wait until I was done with the realtor and so I could have a chance to explain things to my wife. The sheriff waited in my driveway blockading my car in the garage with the tow truck. Wow what a day; three unrelated attacks that tore our life apart all in one day. This officially has become the worst 24 hour period in our lives. But things seemed to continue down a dark road a little further before the light began to emerge.

Handcuffs can restrict blood flow

However, the hardest part was being arrested. This almost makes it sound like I am some sort of criminal, but what I later realized is that this experience put me in some pretty good company – Nelson Mandela, the Apostle Paul, Jesus and many other innocent men who were living out the truth in their lives.

Due to a misunderstanding I was being charged for driving a motor vehicle without an operator's license. My license was taken away due to that financial dispute with my ex-wife yet I still needed to drive for my (already struggling) business. So I wrote a letter to the police superintendent, his boss and the minister of transportation explaining the situation and asked them to notify me if I was offside. Rather than a response back I was set up and arrested. So here I found myself trying to explain my situation to a "peace" officer. He did not care to try and understand what it was that I was saying and all the documentation that I had already sent his boss and was trying to explain to him. He interpreted my frustration as aggressiveness which in turn led him and his partner to throw me to the ground and with a knee in the back and my face pressed into the ground I had the handcuffs slapped on. My step kids and wife watched with tears in their eyes confused and disturbed. And during the whole ordeal I was slandered and shouted at as being a "dumb ass" and could not explain to them what was happening. I was hauled away to spend a good part of the night behind bars. Sitting in the cell I was helpless and could not comfort those who just witnessed my demeaning arrest.

As a result of this embarrassing, humiliating and exhausting night my ex wife withheld my children, feeling that they were not safe with me. I spent the next several days trying to contact them and let them know that everything was going to be ok. But all they saw was that their dad was a convict. They were hearing a lot of negative words spoken about me and I was not able to give them a hug and explanation. And while all of this was happening, my business had been suffering which had caused all sorts of financial pressures and my marriage with LJ was on life support just hanging by a thread.

What hope did I hang on to during this time? In the New Testament in the letter that Jesus's little brother James wrote, is a very cool promise. It says:

"Dear brothers and sisters, whenever trouble comes your way let it be an opportunity for Joy! For when your faith is tested your endurance will grow. So let it grow... for when your endurance is fully developed, you will be strong in character and ready for anything."

Wow! It's a deal. If the outcome can be a strong character and preparation for any further future challenges, then I will continue pushing forward.

So I share all this for one reason. I want you to understand that regardless of the troubles and trials that you are facing, the end of your story can be filled with hope and a miracle. The end of my story takes a complete 180 and that is what has made these last few years much easier to bear. I learned some things that I wouldn't have if it weren't for these troubles and trials:

- I finally learned how to be faithful with the things God has already blessed me with. I have been blessed with a second chance of being married to an amazing woman and a growing love that we share. I have already messed up in some big ways in not honoring and loving LJ the way that God has called me to. Yet we have passed some tests and grown stronger.

- I have allowed myself to fall prey to the lies of our 'consumption' society by buying things that shouldn't have been such a priority. So this resulted in debt beyond what I would have thought I was capable of. I was a slave to so many and I did this all willingly and became buried. And why? Because I did not have the self control and wisdom to say No! It says very clearly in the Bible that we are to be a slave to no man and when we have a debt to someone that they become our master and therefore we are their servants. I had not been a great steward with the finances that I had been blessed with.

- I also learned about living a life of discipline rather than regret. Every day I run the race to take me closer to my goal. The longer I sit on the sidelines the further away from the finish line I stray. I want to finish the race and hear the words:

"Well done my good and faithful servant"!!

(this is the only time I will take pleasure in being called a servant.)

I began a journey of renewing and repairing my relationship with LJ and putting her needs ahead of my own just like I had always known I should be doing. I also started to dig myself out of the debt hole that I dug. And God started to bless my business with some surprises. And this was the beginning of the freedom that I had been seeking.

But you will have to wait until the 2nd half to read in more detail about some of the ridiculous truths that I discovered and blessings that I have encountered. First I want to share with you a little history that has created the world that we live in today.

A History Lesson

In order to better understand all of the poor decisions it is essential to first understand some of the background of how humanity got to this point in the first place. All through history we have been plagued by leaders who have not led with the best interest of the people in mind but have had their own political agendas. They have made decisions which served the small, elite minority rather than the masses. Because of this corruption, it is tough to know how far back to go in order to give a grand picture of where we are at today.

Because of the rich history and global power of the USA, a lot of the history and examples are US based. Because of our (Canadian) proximity and close relationship with them, their history affects us more than you may realize. Here are a few key times in history that have contributed to the slavery that we are living in today:

3000 BC

The Israelites were no longer content with having judges in place and instead wanted a king to rule over them like the other nations around. They no longer understood and appreciated the true value of having God as their King and wanted a human king. God warned them that this would cause lots of problems, that a human king will claim rights to things that no man should claim: "he will take your children and make them serve him (the army), he will take your property for his benefit (lack of property rights), he will take a tenth of your flocks and your grain (income tax – wish it was only 10%) and he will make you his slaves". This account can be referenced in I Samuel chapter 8 in the Bible. Whether you believe the bible or not, it is considered by historians to be an accurate record of history in many respects.

Unfortunately it is normal today to have BIG government (regardless whether we call it democracy or not) and to follow a corrupt system that does not have the people's best interests in mind. We can't even comprehend what it would be like to not have men/women ruling in roles of power. But this is how it used to be. There were judges that were in positions of ruling on God's behalf. There were no kings, presidents, prime ministers, premiers, governors or mayors.

So now we can jump forward to the 1900s where millenniums of corrupt leaders have twisted things to the point where there have been wars over things that should have been settled without bloodshed, laws that have been made that weren't intended to protect the people but rather benefit the elite, and deceit that has been hidden so deep as to keep the people ignorant and content with mediocrity. All of this because the people wanted a king to rule over them.

1910-13

On a late winter evening a small group of leaders gathered in a place called Jekyll Island to make some decisions which would affect the world for the next century. They decided to form a bank that would determine the direction of the world super power's finances and monetary policy– they called it the Federal Reserve Bank. The basic idea of trying to centralize the local banks' lending had merit. But since lying, deceit, fraud, corruption, false testimony and wickedness described the lives of this banking elite, it also defines the institution which they gave birth to. This small elite group has benefited beyond belief and the masses have suffered by this deceptive control. This continued into events like in 1933 when President Roosevelt confiscated (nationalized) all the gold because the country's reserves were running low. So now commerce could no longer be done in real money, essentially at this point the US had declared bankruptcy and now the collateral that was used to back the country's debt was the labor of the people. Birth certificates were now issued in order to monetize and secure the debt that would eventually become all consuming and owed to an evil central banking system on a global scale. This would set the stage for a legalized slavery system where the public would voluntarily apply and feel grateful for the opportunity.

As Canadians we do not have a Federal Reserve Bank. We instead have the Bank of Canada. It is a different system but has the same fundamental flaws and is controlled by the same group of international banksters. The Bank of Canada has not been fulfilling its mandate since 1974 when they allowed the private banks to step in to the position of creating the majority of our country's money. According to information on Wikipedia amongst several other sources http://en.wikipedia.org/wiki/Bank_of_Canada the private banks issues 95% of Canada's money through fractional reserve banking (banks loaning out money beyond what they actually have on deposit). And as I mentioned before the banks do not lend out their money. They simply create credit and put people on the hook to repay this fraudulent loan transaction. Because of this, our country is in debt to the private banksters rather than our own bank. And this has resulted in the need to pay interest and gargantuan debt payments to the banksters instead of being able to internally control it. On top of all this, in 2008 the Bank of Canada also took part in a secret bailout helping out the five big banks. If you look at the profitability of these banks and then look at how our Bank felt the need to bail them out with tax payer money, then you realize that there is a fundamental flaw in our system.

At this exact second of writing this chapter, the national debt for Canada is at $609,997,959,145 according to http://www.debtclock.ca. I encourage you to check on the debt yourself as you finish this paragraph and see how much it has grown. I better hurry and finish this; it just grew to $609,998,358,346 and that was just after a few minutes.

Fred Van Liew

<u>1971</u>

No longer was there such a concept as a balanced budget. Deficits were going to be the norm. Every year the deficits would grow and the debt explode. And then President Nixon finished it off when he pulled the remainder of the dollar off the gold standard; this was the end of sound money. Canada followed the same trend as did every country in the world. So the debt would grow which would create the need for more paper money printing which would in turn create inflationary pressure and therefore higher interest rates and in full circle larger deficits and greater mountains of debt.

This was the point where there could now be an unlimited amount of the fiat currency available. Throughout history there have been over 3800 fiat currencies that have all failed with a 30-40 year average life expectancy. But today is the first time in history where every country in the world are all using a fiat currency; no longer having a gold or silver backing. Whenever necessary more paper can be printed to temporarily correct a financial mess. It has allowed countries to cover over problems rather than solving them. This is the Keynesian approach to economics. Rather than admitting that there is a problem and addressing it, they try to solve the problem with BIG government and massive amounts of currency printing. By the time the consequences of these actions are an issue, our generation will be long gone and our kids' generation is left to deal with the problems. This is just like the patient who has gangrene in his toe. The doctor books him for surgery saying that he needs to amputate his toe. But instead the patient insists that he will get better so gets discharged with a band aid on his toe. Not long after the gangrene has spread to his foot. He has a tensor bandage wrapped around his foot and continues as normal. Suddenly he finds that the gangrene has spread to his knee. The doctor shakes his head and tries to convince his patient that he has no choice but to amputate his leg from the knee down. Again the stubborn and ignorant patient just requests bandages and a quick discharge. Eventually he is consumed with the gangrene and his life is over. It all could have been resolved with a fairly simple amputation of his toe and he could have easily adjusted to life minus a toe. But instead he chose death in the long term. This is the direction that countries such as the USA are headed.

This is the point in history where inflation became a factor. Before this prices remained quite constant and now they would increase on average of 2-4% per year (which is what the government considers to be healthy). At the time of writing this book the dollar has lost over 95% of its value since 1971 – not far to go until it is worth-less.

As a student of history I have learned a lot about where we have gone wrong and the impact that these brutal turn of events have had on present day life. If any of the above brief points have created further questions, I encourage you to go to http://www.freedomPS.ca/debt-and-taxes/
where you can find several links that will give further explanation.

Action

If there is something from this chapter that got your attention that you either want to look further into or something that you want to put into practice in your life take a couple notes:

A Head on Collision with Fraud

Chapter 3

Most of the time I am quite healthy; I get sick about once a year and even then only for a day or two. But for those 24-48 hours I become very thankful for my health. Most of the time I take my health for granted – I may eat unhealthy, I become somewhat lethargic, I forget to take my vitamins. When people age, health can slip in such a gradual decline and then "poof", suddenly one is dealing with ailments and illnesses that seem impossible to heal.

The same thing happens to our freedom. We take it for granted and slowly let outside forces creep in and slowly and gradually we start walking down a road forgetting the freedoms that we were born with. It doesn't help that there is a much stronger tug pulling us towards bondage especially during times of economic upheaval. As I am writing this book, there is a great uncertainty in the world as where things are headed. It seems likely that things could get much worse before they get better.

History shows us that when governments start to get into financial trouble, their only solution is to try to control and regulate everything. They impose capital controls, wage and price controls, exchange controls, border and travel controls, and population controls. They destroy freedom in the name of preserving the status quo. I have struggled whether to include this chapter or not due to its controversial content. But over the last few months I have watched the stories of government corruption unfold and realized that we are heading down a very dark road. I have realized that you need to consider what I am about to share with you whether you agree with it or not.

I am aware that the 80/20 rule may apply here. 80% of you may just dismiss this chapter and form a prejudgment based on your past learning and experience. I encourage you to read this section with an open mind. If after some of your own research you come to a different conclusion, then at least you are informed and not basing your conclusions on the ignorant assumptions of the masses. I strongly believe that the time will come when the truth will become clearer and that many of you will recognize it. I have spent years wrestling with these ideas and still find myself perplexed; I hope that you will do some wrestling as well. There is a freedom that I want you to experience beyond all of these layers. At the end of the chapter I have a list of resources that you can research further as well.

Bill of Rights

Who does Canada's charter apply to? Does it give me my rights? Are all the statutes, bills, acts and laws that fall under it meant to try and govern a man or is this misleading? This is foundational so a good place to begin with a clear understanding.

"This charter applies to the Parliament and government of Canada in respect of all matters within the authority of Parliament..."

--Article 32 of the Canadian Charter of Rights and Freedoms

I am not an employee of the government of Canada nor am I a Member of Parliament. If you look at the Bill of Rights that Diefenbaker signed in 1960 freedom is truly declared:

"I am a Canadian, a free Canadian, free to speak without fear, free to worship God in my own way, free to stand for what I think right, free to oppose what I believe wrong, free to choose those who shall govern my country. This heritage of freedom I pledge to uphold for myself and all mankind."

It does not say that it only applies to Parliament. It was written for the people. The freedom that it declares can not simply be ended by the writing of another document which intends control. This freedom is our heritage and a gift from God that can not be taken away. But we can voluntarily give it away if we choose.

We need to reprogram and adjust our thinking in regards to a lot of what we have grown accustomed to and thought of as normal. Our rights are God given and not given to us from the government. And therefore, they can only be taken away by God. This is not a role that the government should be playing – they should not be trying to control our lives. Their role was intended to be public servants, not to rule over us and create a system of servitude. We have grown so far away from this that we do not even recognize the insanity.

The Birth Certificate

It all starts at birth with registration. Just as we register our vehicles as property we are also forced to register our children.

This is one hospital visit that is both exciting and very overwhelming all at the same time. The experience of having children is one that is not easily forgotten. Once your beautiful miracle has been born, then the fun begins with the paperwork. Now you must register this young, innocent child so that they can receive a certificate of live birth. Have you ever known someone who has tried to leave the hospital with their baby without filling this paperwork out? Your baby is held hostage until this is done; they do not want any children without registration into their system. Does this not sound a little like forced slavery? The very process of mandatory registration of anything implies to me that one is giving up ownership and control.

If the child is yours why are you being forced to apply for something where there is not full disclosure and understanding? Ignorance. As long as we don't understand and don't ask too many questions then they can continue to get away with it.

Many of the quotes that I will be citing are from U.S politicians and many of the numbers are based on U.S. statistics. This applies to us here equally in Canada and is very pertinent due to our extremely close ties with our neighbors to the south.

"[Very] soon, every American will be required to register their biological property in a National system designed to keep track of the people and that will operate under the ancient system of pledging. By such methodology, we can compel people to submit to our agenda, which will affect our security as a chargeback for our fiat paper currency. Every American will be forced to register or suffer not being able to work and earn a living. They will be our chattel, and we will hold the security interest over them forever, by operation of the law merchant under the scheme of secured transactions. Americans, by unknowingly or unwittingly delivering the bills of lading to us will be rendered bankrupt and insolvent, forever to remain economic slaves through taxation, secured by their pledges. They will be stripped of their rights and given a commercial value designed to make us a profit and they will be none the wiser, for not one man in a million could ever figure our plans and, if by accident one or two would figure it out, we have in our arsenal plausible deniability. After all, this is the only logical way to fund government, by floating liens and debt to the registrants in the form of benefits and privileges. This will inevitably reap to us huge profits beyond our wildest expectations and leave every American a contributor or to this fraud which we will call "Social Insurance." Without realizing it, every American will insure us for any loss we may incur and in this manner; every American will unknowingly be our servant, however begrudgingly. The people will become helpless and without any hope for their redemption and, we will

employ the high office of the President of our dummy corporation to foment this plot against America."

Edward Mandell House had this to say in a private meeting with Woodrow Wilson (Pres. 1913-1921)

100 years ago they knew what they were doing – they were creating a system that the masses wouldn't question. Control is the agenda and most are satisfied as long as their needs are met. If you Google "birth certificate a sign of slavery" you will have ample reading to give you a better understanding.

On a phone call with Vital Statistics I was told that the birth certificate is not intended to be a form of ID. But in order to get any government issued ID, the birth certificate is required. Stop right now and go get your birth certificate, SIN card or drivers license. Look at how your name is written. When you learned to write your name you wrote it with the first letter capitalized and the remaining letters small case – Douglas Loewen. But on your government identification your name will mostly be written in UPPER CASE. Do some of your own research – start with some online law dictionaries and this is what you will find:

Capitis Diminutio *(meaning the diminishing of status through the use of capitalization) In Roman law. A diminishing or abridgment of personality; a loss or curtailment of a man's status or aggregate of legal attributes and qualifications.*

Capitis Diminutio Minima *(meaning a minimum loss of status through the use of capitalization, e.g. John Doe) - The lowest or least comprehensive degree of loss of status. This occurred where a man's family relations alone were changed. It happened* *upon the arrogation [pride] of a person who had been his own master, (sui juris,) [of his own right, not under any legal disability] or upon the emancipation of one who had been under the patria potestas. [Parental authority] It left the rights of liberty and citizenship unaltered. See Inst. 1, 16, pr.; 1, 2, 3; Dig. 4, 5, 11; Mackeld. Rom.Law, 144.*

Capitis Diminutio Media *(meaning a medium loss of status through the use of capitalization, e.g. John DOE) - A lesser or medium loss of status. This occurred where a man loses his rights of citizenship, but without losing his liberty. It carried away also the family rights.*

Capitis Diminutio Maxima *(meaning a maximum loss of status through the use of capitalization, e.g. JOHN DOE or DOE JOHN) - The highest or most comprehensive loss of status. This occurred when a man's condition was changed from one of freedom to one of bondage, when he became a slave. It swept away with it all rights of citizenship and all family rights.*

It is important to understand the purpose of the birth certificate. Is it a form of ID as we have all assumed or is it deceitfully intended for monetization of debt? I am still looking for some conclusive evidence to lead me to the truth.

<u>SIN</u>

When a government offers a social security program to its people it is important to understand at what cost. What needs to be sacrificed in order to enjoy this benefit? In 1964 when the social insurance program was introduced in Canada it was attached to the need for a 9 digit social insurance number. Initially this was used to help administer

CPP, then three years later it was attached and also used for tax identification purposes. It became an ordinary part of growing up. I remember applying for mine when I was 15 years old – I never understood what I was doing. All I knew was that in order for me to be able to flip burgers at McDonalds for $3.30/hr I needed to have the SIN. Now parents are applying for SINs for their children when they are infants so that they can qualify for education grants. What is their agenda here?

On the Service Canada website it says that "the SIN is a 9 digit # that you need to work in Canada or receive government benefits". Read this again to understand the wording. Is it saying that anyone who works in Canada must have a SIN? My understanding is that if you either want to have access to government programs and benefits or work in Canada then you must have a SIN. I have forfeited these benefits and have learned not to count on them for any sort of future planning.

Inside the Box

Unless you are a baby boomer don't plan for CPP as a part of your retirement planning. According to CBC the ratio of workers to retirees has decreased from 17:1 in 1950 to 2.2:1 by 2050. You may pay into this your entire working life and end up having little to nothing in the end.

Get educated and invest for your future

Governments are very careful in their choice of words; they have gone as far as changing definitions of words to suit their needs. If they had intended to communicate that citizens need a SIN to work and collect government benefits then they would have used "and" instead of "or". Refer back to the previous Edward Mandell House quote: *"Every American will be forced to register or suffer not being able to work and earn a living"*. This definitely seems like their intent.

In order to buy or sell anything apparently I need this identification number... or in our case - in order to work and earn a living you need the SIN. I continue to struggle with this.

<u>Inflation</u>

"Inflation is as violent as a mugger, as frightening as an armed robber and as deadly as a hit man."

Ronald Reagan

How would life be different if there wasn't any inflation? Generally wages do not keep up with the increased cost of living. This has caused many families to have no other choice than for both parents to have to go to work and leave the children without supervision. As the discrepancy between income and cost of living has continually increased eventually the only other choice has been to borrow in order to survive. And this is where we are at today. Again, this has created a situation where the majority of families are living as slaves to the bank and their country.

Also consider that the Capital Gains Tax is applied when you sell an asset that has increased in value. How often have these assets appreciated in value due to your dollar actually having lost value. Is this something that you should be taxed on? Inflation is already a hidden tax. It is a shame to have to pay a capital gains tax on top of your currency losing its value.

I met with a financial advisor last week who told me that he was thankful that inflation has been so minimal these last several years. I didn't know what to say... I wanted to strip him of his accreditation; people go to financial planners and trust them for their advice. Hearing that inflation has been minimal when in actuality it has been very high may mislead clients into making poor financial decisions.

I recently read an article on the Huffington post of the Eleven Lies about the Federal Reserve Bank; one of which was that Quantitative Easing does not cause inflation. It went on to say that in 2012 inflation was kept to 1.4% which was considered a success since the Fed's target is 2%.

In 1994 the government changed how they calculated inflation. No longer would they include food, energy and housing due to their volatility. This allows them to only modestly increase their government benefits that are indexed to inflation on an annual basis rather than being forced to increase them in proportion to the real cost of living increase. Any time that a government is skewing the facts and hiding the truth, it is important to try and understand their hidden agenda.

If they were using the same methods to calculate inflation today as they did in the 1970s when inflation was hitting 10-12% and causing protests; today inflation would actually be pegged at 9.6% rather than the estimated 2%.

A friend of mine found an old 2006 menu from a local restaurant so compared prices to the 2012 costs for the exact same items.

Clucks n' Greens increased by 30.5%
Fish n' Chips increased by 38.9%
A Hamburger increased by 24.5%
Chicken wings increased by 31.1%

This doesn't look like a 2% average annual inflation rate. What a great way to control the masses. Manipulate their understanding and therefore their perspective on reality. Then the government has control over how people react to factors that are outside of their control.

Newsmax reported that from 2009-2011 the prices of food soared on average by 57%, the price of fuel 34 % and the cost of cotton skyrocketed 210%. The time is coming where these basics become unaffordable and more items of luxury that can only be afforded by the rich.

In the Economic Collapse blog Michael Snyder explains why inflation hasn't hit exorbitant records yet. He mentions that the Federal Reserve has printed trillions of dollars but that they are paying the banks not to lend this money out. The U.S. banks are holding on to $1.8T which is 1000 times more than what they had in their reserves in 2008. When this money starts pouring into the economy it will have a devastating effect; there will be a tsunami of inflation.

2000 years ago during the time of Christ 1 oz of gold would buy a nice robe, tunic, leather belt and a pair of sandals. Today an oz of gold will still buy a decent suit, belt and pair of shoes. Gold and silver maintain their purchasing power whereas your paper currency does not.

Inside the Box

It is essential to your family's survival that you understand the true devaluation of your currency and are saving real money (gold and silver) as well. The monopoly paper in your wallet is just a currency that will die as every other of the 3800+ fiat currencies have. Gold and silver will continue to be recognized as money (still as defined in the Coinage Act of 1792) as they always have throughout history.

Buy as much silver as you can today.

"Only government can take perfectly good paper, cover it with perfectly good ink, and make the combination worthless."

Milton Friedman

<u>Income Tax</u>

The majority of income taxes collected are directed towards the payment of our national debt which has been funded by private international bankers who have simply created the credit. It's completely and utterly fraudulent. Consider then that the CRA and IRS agencies are essentially the collection arms for the central banks that a country's debt is owed to. Just as you owe debt to the gang-banksters, so does almost every government around the world. The difference is that the government has a plan for servicing their debt. They strong arm their citizens into a position where our arms are tied and in order to earn a living, we need to first pay for this debt and then with what is left over we can feed our family. Tax Freedom Day is the time of the year that one has to work in order to have all of his/her taxes paid. From that day on, your annual taxes are paid and your earnings are to take care of your family.

Country	Days of Yr	% of Burden	Date of Yr
United States	99	26.9%	9 April
Australia	112	30.7%	22 April
United Kingdom	150	40.9%	30 May
Canada	157	42.6%	6 June
Germany	190	51.7%	8 July
Belgium	217	59.2%	5 August

For almost half of the year our earnings are to pay the banksters for a fraudulent debt and a BIG government to rule and pretend to be public servants.

Just to be clear, I am not suggesting any sort of tax evasion. We have chosen to live in this country so we also need to follow its laws whether they make sense or not. I have personally tried a few different 'out of the box' tax strategies and they take a lot of energy to understand and defend. So I caution you to tread lightly when it comes to how to handle your relationship with the CRA/IRS! My suggestion is that you learn the difference between tax avoidance and tax evasion and find someone who can help you lawfully avoid as much income tax as possible.

<u>Inside the Box</u>

From reading the book <u>10 Secrets Revenue Canada Doesn't Want You To Know</u>, I would encourage everyone to learn how to convert the interest on your mortgage to being deductible, how to use a small business to utilize tax deductions effectively and to maximize the power of charitable giving.

In 1974 when Trudeau changed the country's debt from being public to being private, this put the banksters in a position of collecting a ginormous amount of interest on the backs of the taxpayer.

A 1993 Auditor General report said that of the accumulated net debt of $423 billion, only $37 billion was principal - the rest was due to the magic of compound interest.

In 2011-2012, CRA collected about $419 billion in taxes and duties. The Canadian government debt hit $600Billion in November 2012 and approximately 80% of this debt is a result of compounding interest.

The Banksters

Most Canadians have a mortgage and think of their house as an asset. Your house is not an asset; if it's not putting money into your pocket then it is a liability. The root word of "mortgage" is the Latin word for death pledge – that should give us enough to walk away but instead most of us will at one time or another have had one of these death pledges. Why is it so acceptable in our society to have a mortgage when we are paying up to three times the value of our house to the banksters in interest payments? I have some interesting experience when it comes to questioning the banks on the mortgage. It has had some cost but the things that I have learned have been mind blowing/numbing. You need to make a choice whether you want to continue to trust the banks with your future. Do they really have your best interest in mind? Or do they have an agenda that is serving their best interests? Absofreakinlutely! If you look at who is leading our country and how these bankers' agendas have affected things, then you will realize that you can no longer entrust your life to these people's control.

First of all, what is it that they are lending you? Are they taking assets off their balance sheet and loaning it to you so you can make your purchase? In order for a loan to be legitimate, there needs to be some loss/risk from the lending party. It is becoming common knowledge that this is not the case. It's called fractional reserve banking; the bank loans what they do not have. They are just creating credit. It is a debt based system that is not based on money at all. When I asked a billionaire out of Australia what he thought of our western world system of banking he described it as legalized fraud; he said "there is no right way to do the wrong thing". And this is precisely what our banks have been doing for the last 100 years... and why the foundations of our economies are on the brink of total financial collapse.

Just take a look at our money (or should I say currency). If you have a bill in your pocket, take a look at it right now. It is called a note. A promissory note is a promise to pay which is equivalent to debt. Our currency is actually debt – it is not backed by anything other than a promise. This allows the banks to print an infinite amount of the fiat paper which causes inflation – I covered this in the last chapter. This is a modern day equivalent of the ancient Roman practice of shaving the edges of coins to cheat the people quietly.

In June 2011 the Federal Reserve was audited and they found that there was $16 Trillion in secret bailouts without congress support. These bailouts were given to many domestic and international banks. Since the Fed is not a body of the government but instead a private bank run by a small group of international banksters, it should give a hint that their agenda may not be in the best interest of the people. This can be found on the senator of Vermont's website among many other places. As mentioned previously, Canada is in the same position with bailing out the big banks.

So the question is – if what they are doing is wrong, where does that leave us, the debtors? Is there any way of seeing justice? Still working on it…hope to get this worked out!!!

Here are some quotes that drive this home. It is essential that we learn from those who have walked before us. I am sure that our Canadian Prime Ministers would have echoed the sentiments of these US leaders.

It is well enough that people of the nation do not understand our banking and monetary system, for if they did, I believe there would be a revolution before tomorrow morning.
Henry Ford

Give me control of a nation's money and I care not who makes her laws.
Mayer Amschel Rothschild

The modern banking system manufactures money out of nothing.
Banking was conceived in iniquity and born in sin. The bankers own the earth.
But if you want to continue to be slaves of the banks and pay the cost of your own slavery, then let bankers continue to create money and control credit.
Josiah Stamp Banker in England in 1920's and second richest man in Britain

"The few who understand the system, will either be so interested from it's profits or so dependant on it's favours, that there will be no opposition from that class."

Rothschild Brothers of London, 1863

"The Federal Reserve banks are one of the most corrupt institutions the world has ever seen. There is not a man within the sound of my voice who does not know that this nation is run by the International bankers." –

Congressman Louis T. McFadden (Rep. Pa)

"I am a most unhappy man. I have unwittingly ruined my country. A great industrial nation is controlled by it's system of credit. Our system of credit is concentrated in the hands of a few men. We have come to be one of the worst ruled, one of the most completely controlled and dominated governments in the world-- no longer a government of free opinion, no longer a government by conviction and vote of the majority, but a government by the opinion and duress of small groups of dominant men." –

President Woodrow Wilson –approved the Federal Reserve Bank in 1913

"We are completely dependant on the commercial banks. Someone has to borrow every dollar we have in circulation, cash or credit. If the banks create ample synthetic money we are prosperous; if not, we starve. We are absolutely without a permanent money system.... It is the most important subject intelligent persons can investigate and reflect upon. It is so important that our present civilization may collapse unless it becomes widely understood and the defects remedied very soon." –

Robert H. Hamphill, Atlanta Federal Reserve Bank

"This [Federal Reserve Act] establishes the most gigantic trust on earth. When the President [Wilson} signs this bill,

the invisible government of the monetary power will be legalized....the worst legislative crime of the ages is perpetrated by this banking and currency bill." – "From now on, depressions will be scientifically created." –

Charles A. Lindbergh, Sr., 1913

"The financial system has been turned over to the Federal Reserve Board. That Board administers the finance system by authority of a purely profiteering group. The system is Private, conducted for the sole purpose of obtaining the greatest possible profits from the use of other people's money"

Charles A. Lindbergh Sr., 1923

"I believe that banking institutions are more dangerous to our liberties than standing armies. Already they have raised up a monied aristocracy that has set the government at defiance. The issuing power (of money) should be taken away from the banks and restored to the people to whom it properly belongs." –

Thomas Jefferson, U.S. President.

"When you or I write a check there must be sufficient funds in our account to cover the check, but when the Federal Reserve writes a check there is no bank deposit on which that check is drawn. When the Federal Reserve writes a check, it is creating money."

Boston Federal Reserve Bank

"There's a plot in this country to enslave every man, woman and child. Before I leave this high and noble office I intend to expose this plot."

JFK -7 days before his assassination

God created man. Man then decided to create the government. And the government started the banks. This is the natural order of creation which should in turn determine the direction of control.

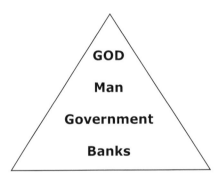

But today in reality things are completely upside down. The banksters control the government. The government tries to control the people. And GOD is pushed to the bottom. This is not the order of creation and needs to be changed.

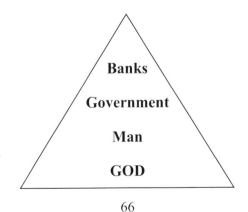

Below is a picture of the amount of derivative exposure that the banks have created in the USA. As of 2010 there was a total $228 Trillion that the nine largest banks have accumulated. These are stacks of pallets of $100 bills.

demonocracy.info

On top of that, there is a multi Trillion dollar deficit that continues to climb and when totaling unfunded liabilities it is well over $100 Trillion and according to some even up to $200 Trillion.

This is where the majority of people have a good portion of their retirement sitting. Do you wake up in the middle of the night wondering if it is still there?

If for the last 2000 years since the time of Christ the Roman government spent $1 Million each and everyday, then today Rome would have approximately $735 Billion of debt. Not really that bad considering their reality.

Another picture that will help you to understand the enormity of the financial mess is that $1M weighs 22 lbs. My nine year old could easily carry a Mil to school in her backpack. But if you were to weigh a Trillion dollars, it would weigh 11,000 Tons. In order to haul this you would need well over 200 semi trailers.

Since I am a visual learner, I have to leave you with one more picture. If you stacked up $100 bills, $1Million would be just a bit over 4 feet tall. $1Billion would be 4166 feet high. And $1Trillion would be 789 miles high. If you took the estimated $200Trillion that some estimate the US government's total debt at, that would be a stack of $100 bills two thirds the distance to the moon. Canada's pile would be 773 km high; this goes beyond the earth's atmosphere which is out of this world!!!

All of this to say that the banks have created a problem that can not be solved. The only answer is one that will bring a lot of suffering and years of turmoil that the people will pay for.

I realize that all of the quotes that I have used are from other world leaders so I thought that we should have at least one good Canadian PM give us some parting words:

"Until the control of the issue of currency and credit is restored to the government and recognized as its most

sacred responsibility, all talk of the sovereignty...is idle and futile."

William Lyon MacKenzie, PM of Canada 1934

<u>Choose Your Law</u>

In the movie <u>First Knight</u>, King Arthur AKA Sean Connery says in a very convicted tone and cool Scottish accent,

"There are laws that enslave men and then there are laws that set them free".

I would go as far as to say that the main purpose of man's law/statutes is to enslave and control men whereas God's law is to set us free. How can we follow both? If they contradict each other are we not forced to make a choice? But I stress that you need to use a lot of wisdom and discernment as this is where I have followed my heart and didn't use my head to make wise decisions where my family was concerned.

Once you understand the facts that each of us has lived our whole lives believing, then it becomes easier to take a step outside of the box and see the same thread weaving through it all. It is possible to understand the truth, to be convicted of the truth, and to live the truth out without being a lunatic "conspirator" or "doomsdayer": The importance is that you take the time to do your own study, determine the path that is right for you and forge ahead with conviction and passion.

Further Reading and Googling

<u>They Own It All (Including You)</u> by Ronald MacDonald

www.infowars.com

http://www.ohcanadamovie.com/

Ron Paul

Max Keiser

Sovereign Man

Action

I hope that I stirred things up a little bit here for you. I encourage you to pick 1-2 areas that you want to look deeper into.

The End of My Story & Beginning of Yours

2nd Half

Before you read any further it is important that you understand where I am coming from. By now if you haven't figured it out; I am a God-fearing and God loving man. I believe that I was created in the image of God, with an intellect, emotions and a will to determine my journey. I believe that my Creator has a plan for me to prosper and succeed. But I know that for me as well as most people, we have strayed far from this perfect plan. Because of these things that I have learned and put to practice my life is now in a great place. At the end of the book I share some examples of what's changing. But rather than focusing any more on my story, I want to begin to help you explore what this all means in the context of your life.

The second half is about how to get back on the path of the perfect plan and discover the freedom that our creator has intended for us.

My hope is for you to learn how to become more free in every area of your life regardless of where your spiritual beliefs are at. So please read on even if we aren't at the same place spiritually.

Who is going to write your next chapter?

I have shared with you some of the difficult lessons that I have learned and my steep learning curve of how I have challenged the paradigms in my own life.

I will share with you some of the victories from my own bondage in specific areas of my life. And then I will challenge you to write your own story and finish it strong.

The Bleeding Continues

Now that I may have messed with the paradigms that you have been raised with, hopefully you still trust that I am sane and my head is not completely filled with thoughts of conspiracy and delusion. I trust that this journey is one that God has led me on and that there will be readers who have had some of the same questions without adequate answers. I have talked with so many where there is a feeling of discontentment, feelings of despair and a shortage of hope. All of this would be a waste of words if there were not a victory at the end of the game.

This is where the light gets really bright and where William Wallace declares:

"Every man dies, not every man really lives".

This is the part of the story that has given me the motivation to write this book. So I am glad that you have stuck with it because we are just getting to the part that matters.

The freedoms that I am experiencing now are beyond what most have experienced and why I have written this book. The intent of this book is to share a message with as many as possible. The next five chapters will focus on living freedom when it comes to your finances, relationships, physical health, your mind and your spirit.

"Just look at us. Everything is backwards. Everything is upside down. Doctors destroy health, lawyers destroy justice, universities destroy knowledge, governments and banks destroy freedom, the major media destroys information and religion destroys spirituality"

Author Unknown

Show me the Money

Chapter 4

Is it possible to live a life of freedom when it comes to your spiritual life, your marriage, your family, your emotional and intellectual life when you still have loads of financial debt and money nightmares?

I thought that this would be possible and I tried this for years while I was still sorting things out trying to get financially healthy.

But I realized that as long as I was in debt that it went against a principle that had been so deeply ingrained in my life that I could not truly be free until I got rid of those chains.

In the book of Proverbs King Solomon compares a slave-master relationship to that of a debtor-creditor. One who is in debt is a slave to the banker. Until this relationship of being in debt is abolished nobody can truly live a life of absolute freedom. It goes against who we were designed to be and how we were created to live.

I have also been challenged by another truth that is written in the book of Proverbs. It says that when we trust in God with everything, no longer depending on our limited understanding and seek him in everything that He will show us which path to take. In regards to money, either when I have had loads of debt or cash in my wallet, I have had a difficult time trusting my creator. Until I figured out how to not be anxious about these things but instead be filled with peace, I could not find this beautiful freedom.

So that is why the starting point is your financial health. It's not that finances are the central most important thing in my life. But as long as you are financially sick it can bleed into every other area in our lives and no matter how hard we try we may remain in bondage in these other areas.

If you are in debt right now you like most other people on this planet have gone against the design of how you were created and you will not truly live your life to its full potential until this has been resolved.

I have heard and truly agree that finances and family are the two most common stressors between a husband and wife. Sometimes there's not a lot we can do about family tension but financial strain can often be minimized if we take the time to understand where we have strayed off the path.

We have all been lied to and deceived. Those we have trusted and counted on have not been there for us with our best interests in mind. They have been there to make money off our backs. They have been there to line their own pockets with our hard work. They have been there to take advantage of us and use their position and trusted status to milk us for everything that we have.

I have had a business in the financial sector for over a decade now and have learned more about the truth of what is happening than I thought was possible. Instead of going into a ton of detail I am going to paint a broad picture giving just enough information and resources that you can do your own research in the areas that grab your attention.

Here are some things that tick me off in the financial industry. I am going to pick on the banks specifically. When you go into your local bank there are many areas of financial advice available for you.

Words of "Wisdom" from your Financial Advisor

Mutual Funds

When it comes time to make your annual contribution to your retirement plan how many of you are sitting with an advisor at the bank? And if so, then you will most likely have been advised to buy some mutual funds and to 'buy and hold'. "Because you have only lost money if you sell" – regardless of where the price of the fund is headed. And then for the portion of your investments that you do not want much risk they have suggested bonds or fixed income. Sorry if this sounds too familiar and you have already lost money following this advice.

As well, with mutual funds it is imperative that you factor in the MERs (Management Expense Ratio). Once you pay the mutual fund manager and your advisor their annual fees what is left for you? Who is holding all the risk? And who is getting paid first regardless of whether the fund makes any money or not? The answers to these questions should be enough for you to run away right now.

A mutual fund has been sold as the ultimate tool of diversification. The problem is that it is only diversifying you in one sector (the stock market) so when another 2008 hits, regardless of your diversification you will take another big hit. This would be similar to investing your entire real estate portfolio all on the same block of residential single family blue houses with attached garages and white picket fences. True diversification would insulate you from these downturns. Another secret of the wealthy is to become a student of wealth cycles so that you are investing in the right sector at the right time rather than following the masses and being run over by the fear and greed freight trains. One answer is not to diversify across every sector because as Warren Buffet says:

"**Diversification** is protection against ignorance. It makes little sense if you know what you are doing."

Take a look at how much money has been made/lost in mutual funds since 2000 and then ask yourself why you are even listening to this hogwash. Go to www.globefund.com and calculate what your mutual fund's ROI has been since inception. I have found the average return to be around 5%; once you factor in the income tax that you will owe and the actual inflation rate you have a negative return. You need 10% + returns in order to take any positive steps forward.

The bond market is also going to have a few challenges. With an average bond rate of 1-5%, it is impossible to get ahead when inflation is already 8-9% and climbing. Your only guarantee is that you will lose money. The other factor that your advisor probably isn't telling you is that since you are investing in debt, the risk is whether the debtor will be able to honor its obligation to pay back principal and the agreed return. If you look at how the Federal Reserve is buying back $85 billion in bonds each month, you can see that there is a lot of debt (bonds) that is too risky for consumers. It is only a matter of time before we see more cities like Detroit declaring bankruptcy, followed by states and provinces and eventually nations. If you have invested in bonds of a municipality or nation that goes broke, your money gets wiped out. As I am writing this, it was just reported that investors pulled out $80 billion out of the bond markets last month (June 2013).

We have already seen how bubbles can wipe out investors (stock market and real estate bubbles popped in 2008). The next bubble to pop will be the largest of them all and that is the bond market bubble.

One of the wealthiest families in the world today is the Rothschild family. But they will never appear in the Forbes top 50 list for reasons that I have already explained. They focus their investing in three sectors:

1. **Real Estate**
2. **Economies of Rarity (wine, art and gems)**
3. **Stock Market – they treat this like a cold shower (they get in and out quickly)**

I love investing in economies of rarity such as rare gems because they do not go down in value. They only appreciate. My area of expertise is natural fancy colored diamonds. You may perceive this as something that is only available for those who are already extremely wealthy; this is not the case. Take the time to learn; google <u>Colored Diamonds</u> and be fascinated by what you have been missing out on. It's not too late (depending on how soon you are reading this). Take another look at the list of how the wealthy invest. Scale this to fit you and do it! Stop investing like the masses; otherwise you will end up like them ---- broke!

Do you understand the concept of an RRSP? It is a vehicle to defer tax – the only guarantee is that you will pay them one day. You aren't guaranteed that you will be able to retire. Are there other ways to minimize tax? Absolutely! RRSPs are not the best solution for everyone as your banker would have you believe. Registered programs such as RRSP, LIRA, LIRF, TFSAs are the perfect system for the government to be able to control its citizens' wealth and direct it where desired.

Inside the Box

Another benefit for those who are self employed is to use other strategies to decrease your tax and not to have to use RRSPs. Then you have many options to invest in non registered ways. You can invest privately so that the government and bank doesn't control your assets.

Death Pledge

I already gave you the background to the concept of a mortgage. This is another service that the bank loves to offer and who wouldn't? They have a twenty five year + guarantee of cash flow when it didn't cost them a penny to acquire it and it is securitized by your largest asset. I made a promise to my family in 2010 that I will never take out another mortgage ever again. Based on what I have learned it would go against my integrity and character to do so. It would kill me from the inside and it's not worth it (regardless of the fantastic rates that they are offering).

Inside the Box

But if you hold a mortgage in Canada then you need to go to http://www.manulifeone.ca/home/calculator/ and compare what you can save by changing how you finance it. You need to have discipline in order to do this. Email me if you want help.

Credit cards

Whether it's Canadian Tire, Wal-Mart or your bank… they have a special credit card offer and are sometimes waiting at the door for you to sign up. It is the same deal as the mortgage. They are creating credit with your signature and you are paying %$&^ fees if you don't pay it off in time. As of September 2012, 36% of Canadians carry a balance and are paying 12%+ in fees for this service. This again is legalized fraud.

> ### Inside the Box
>
> If you are like many Canadians and have too much high interest debt you have two options. You either make a plan to pay it off (start with the smallest balance card, experience some success and then attack the next one and so on) or you do a debt proposal and negotiate with your creditors. This will impact your credit score but may be worth it in the end. Email me and I can introduce you to someone who can help you decide.

The government extracts the wealth of its citizens through the banking system. The banks and government have colluded together to create this system of slavery. Visit www.freedomPS.ca/debt-and-taxes/ to see some incredible videos that highlight this. Then you will be able to grasp the enormity of the problem that is lying before us.

Taste of Reality

As much as we try to be free sometimes it is very difficult to do so with financial bondage hanging over our heads. Personally in my life I have tried many times to think free, to live free and to act free but as long as I was in financial slavery I couldn't seem to fully take that step.

This affected me the most in my marriage. I knew what was right and there was a desire to change but I seemed to always come back to the fact that I wasn't where I needed to be in regards to my finances.

I am learning how to trust in God and not rely on my own understanding of things. This has been incredible since it has helped me to have a much bigger perspective and vision. I view road blocks and obstacles much differently when I take time to seek God.

Action

Did you learn something for the first time about money? Was there something that grabbed you that you should take some more time to look into?

Hang on to Those You Love

Chapter 5

A past client of mine, Fred, is married to his job. He also has a wife that he is married to with two beautiful children. He already had one close call in his marriage where things were close to over. This gave him a good shakeup, but obviously not enough of a jolt. He continues to this day to put his marriage in third or fourth position. He spends a ridiculous amount of hours working and then is also committed to coaching his kids' sports teams. He is very driven by success which builds his ego and enables him to afford his addiction to toys. At the end of the day he has little to no energy left for his wife. The day will come when he walks in the door to find an empty house and a goodbye note.

Every single one of us is selfish at the core. When it comes to marriage it takes a lot of work to put our spouse's needs first. This is even more difficult when there is financial stress – it's at this point that as a husband I went into survival mode. I would spend more time at my computer crunching numbers, surfing the net looking for the answers, researching the latest opportunities and sometimes just watching useless YouTube videos. Some of these things can be beneficial but never when it's at the expense of our spouse. Now that I have come through the desert I can be honest with myself and with you that the biggest reason that I hid in my man-cave was so I did not have to face those who I knew I was letting down. Wow, that hurts to admit this out loud and in written word. But I need to write this so you can face the truth as well if this is where you are at in your life. This is bondage.

And this is what we need to be freed from. This is the life that our creator wants us to run away from. Now let's look back at how we got here. Most often it starts very subtly and slowly... and innocently. Just spending a little more than you should and not having the discipline that was necessary, not being educated so you could make solid decisions and impulsive decisons! Now that I have been freed from the financial bondage, I have been able to get rid of some handcuffs that did some real damage in my marriage.

Please take a few minutes right now to reflect on the health of your marriage (if you are married) and your relationship with your children and others who are in your community. What is one behavior that you can change?

*turn the TV off and spend time with your spouse

*read to the kids at night and spend some time talking about their day

*turn your computer and cell phone off at supper

*intentionally spend some quality time with friends

*find a hobby to do with your kids or spouse

*recognize any hobby or behavior that is controlling your life and deal with it

Making a Difference

For Christmas 2009 the Super 7 went to the Dominican Republic to meet a part of our family that we had never met before. We began sponsoring 5 children a couple years earlier through Compassion Canada and wanted to meet them and their families. This was an incredible holiday "with a purpose". We were able to bring over 800 pounds of gifts and essential items that we collected from our friends and community; this "blessing" trip was a life changer.

When you are making a difference in other people's lives it is hard to know who is being more impacted, the giver or the receiver. When you experience true and incredible

freedom it is impossible to hold on to it. It begins to bleed from your pores and oozes out of every part of you. Whether you are blessed with an abundance of wealth and are able to give your finances or volunteer some time to help someone in need; taking the time to make a difference is such a blast especially when you do it as a family.

Not only will this have a positive impact on those whom you are helping but it will also improve your relationship with your family. And it will also give you a healthier perspective into your financial health, realizing that you probably are better off than many others around the world. This is a humbling perspective changer that everyone needs to experience.

Recently the Super 7 went on a houseboat trip. I challenged the kids to consider putting together a topic to discuss from the bible. Every night we sat together and took turns leading a "Devo" time where we openly chatted about random things. One of the kids talked about Psalm 23 which you will often hear at funerals. We were hoping that this wasn't foreshadowing in any way. Another discussed the power of our words and how we either speak blessings or curses to each other.

This was an incredible opportunity for our kids to dig deeper into their faith and challenge us.

I encourage you to consider how you can give more opportunity to your family to grow and make a difference in each of their lives and others around you. This will build a concrete foundation that you can stand on together.

Action

Is there something that your family needs you to do in order to be a healthier person?

Is Your Brain a Sponge or a Meteorite?

Chapter 6

Jim was miserable. His days were filled with so much stress that he was at his breaking point. From the pending foreclosure to the bill collectors calling to the utility company threatening to turn off his power; he didn't know how much more he could bear. Every night when he got home he would slouch on the couch with his plate of pizza pops and watch TV until he dozed off into slumber. His mind was not being challenged or exercised at all. He just couldn't bear the thought of reading a book or watching something educational. He really didn't care because he didn't think it would make any difference. What he didn't realize is that the mental rut he was in was making things a whole lot worse. He needed to get some intellectual stimulation or his downward spiral would continue all the way till he hit rock bottom. His mind was as hard as a meteorite; not able to absorb anything beneficial.

The ability to learn is such a beautiful thing that we have been blessed with. If we don't have a desire to learn then our lives will be stagnant and possibly lead to insanity as Einstein defined it; doing the same thing over and over expecting different results. When someone is in bondage they often lack any desire to get out of the rut that they find themselves in. They would rather bathe in self pity and blame others for their circumstances.

I often had a difficult time concentrating while reading a book at bedtime to my children. I went through the actions but after 10 minutes, I had no idea what I had just read. It was challenging when they would ask a question about what we had just finished reading. I had no idea.

I would often fall asleep while watching TV; I had very little capacity to squeeze any more into my brain. I had to make a hard and fast decision that regardless of whether I wanted to or not, I had to spend some time exercising my mind.

I had a difficult time concentrating in a lecture or seminar; I felt like I had ADD. I would leave these feeling as dumb and uninformed as when I started. It was very discouraging.

When I began reading and listening to audio books, I started to see a light at the end of the tunnel. I suddenly felt like I was in the presence of many great authors. I felt like I was being mentored both in my business and personal life by those who I would have never been able to afford otherwise. I had people who loved me encouraging me to read books and listen to podcasts. As I began this discipline, my mind began to expand and soak things up like a sponge.

So instead of being in a rut, I got into a groove. The two positions may not seem all that different but the outcomes are completely opposite. As my life took a 180 degree turn I started to get excited about learning and growing.

Here's a list of some great books that have helped me and I recommend to you:

Financial and Economic

- The Harbinger by Jonathan Cahn
- They Own It All by Ronald McDonald
- Aftershock by David Weidemer
- The Real Crash by Peter Schiff
- Robert Kiyosaki

Living a Successful Life

- The Bible – read one of the books about the life of Jesus to start
- The Richest Man Who Ever Lived by Steven K. Scott
- Success Is Not An Accident by Tommy Newburry
- The 4 Hour Work Week by Tim Ferris
- Anthony Robbins

And others that I have listed directly from Amazon -

Visit http://freedomps.ca/category/achieving-financial-freedom/

<u>Action</u>

Does one of the books appeal to you? What do you need to do in order to experience some brain freedom?

Only Monkeys in Captivity Masturbate.

Chapter 7

Just yesterday we sat with a friend who has lived bound with the chains of being bipolar for years. She shared that she is going in circles and is sick of her guilt and anger being the rulers in her life. In tears she shared how utterly helpless she feels. She feels guilty for not being a great mom to her young daughter. She feels like she has wasted her life. She feels like she has no hope for a better future. As we prayed over her, she just wept and sobbed.

My older brother has struggled with both alcohol and drug abuse for most of his life. I grew up with him being brought to the door by the cops at 3am, breaking a window in the middle of the night because he was too drunk to remember where his house key was, and wrapping dad's car around a light post after a night of partying. At times he has admitted that he has a problem but for the most part he thinks everything is fine. Just recently he said to me "I am tired of a life of always making bad choices". One day we hope to see him stop the madness.

How many people do you see who are not in the physical condition that they once used to be in? Maybe this describes you. When someone is suffering from a life of bondage it is near impossible to be at your prime physically. It is so much easier to slouch on the couch and eat potato chips watching reruns of Seinfeld. This lazy slumber which seems like an easier lifestyle only lasts for a while before the pain digs in.

But rather than the New Year's resolution of getting back to the gym or the new fad diet that guarantees you to lose 40 pounds in the next 40 days, you need to deal with the foundational issues. Until you experience true and lasting freedom, everything else will be fleeting.

In the movie Flight Denzel Washington had been an alcoholic for most of his adult life. Finally he was incarcerated for his neglect as a pilot. While in jail and finally facing his alcoholism head on he declared, "this is the most free that I have ever been". His feeling of freedom was based on the fact that he broke the bondage that alcohol and drugs had and was finally able to embrace life.

If your health is hanging on to the edge of the cliff due to bad choices that you have made, then you need to make a decision right now. You need to let your anger and frustration motivate you to stop the madness. You need to look at the people around you and see the impact that your choices are having on them. You need to taste and smell the sweetness of victory and begin to fight for it. But you may not be able to do this on your own.

Ask your friends and family to hold you accountable to making the necessary changes.

Here are some ideas of positive steps that you can start to take to become free in your physical health:

*Lose some weight.

*Make healthy eating choices. Learn about the ingredients and their impact on your body.

*Exercise – bike or walk to work.

*Find a fun activity with your spouse, kids or a friend to get you moving.

*Go for a walk every night after supper.

*Go to bed at a decent time and get enough sleep.

*Go to a naturopath and get your body in balance.

*Stop the unhealthy habits of over eating, smoking or drinking in excess.

*Limit your TV watching and balance it with exercise.

Action

How are you doing on the physical freedom frontage?
What can you tweak and adjust in order to experience some
tremendous freedom in your body?

Are you a Monk or a Magician?

Chapter 8

I began this book sharing a pseudo fictional story of me growing up with a father who was a king. I wrote this to make a point very clear – that the life we have all been born into may not be the life we are living now. The reason that I call it pseudo fictional is because on a higher level this story is true for all of us. I have remained vague for most of this book because I didn't want you to form an opinion prematurely and shelf the book.

Please hear me out because this is the most important and crucial part of the book and quite possibly of any book that you have ever read. I have shared with you about how financial bondage had affected every area of my life and how I learned to break free from those chains. But the climax is right here! One area of my life that was also in bondage but now is free is that of my Spirit. In our society when we hear the word 'spiritual' many different things come into our minds – this is a word with many different meanings.

To be very clear, the spiritual part of my life that I am referring to is the God-breathed part of me that was created in His image. My goal is to walk this earth with Him in preparation for eternity in His Kingdom and urging as

99

many others along the way to join me on this journey. Our spirits are only to be filled with God and when anything else is substituted there is a deficiency and a void. This is the foundation of who we are. This is the part of each of us that can be in sync with our creator. This is the part of us that will determine the outcome and our next chapter.

I lost a lot of enjoyment in my life due to being in bondage financially and allowing that to determine my spiritual health. I tried to fill my spiritual vacuum with the pleasures that money can buy and it never worked. I encourage you to do things in the right order: fill your Spirit with Jesus Christ and let Him be the centre of your life and allow everything else to fall into place as God allows. Then you aren't putting everything else first trying to fill your void and in search for a freedom that is promising to always be around the next corner but never is.

"Freedom is the oxygen of the soul" is something that Moshe Dayan, a soldier in the Israeli army, said as he was fighting for Israel's freedom in 1948. To me this has an even deeper meaning and something that I have had tattooed on my rib cage as a daily reminder that without this freedom, I am suffocating and having my life choked right out of me. My tattoo is in purple which is symbolic of royalty because I am the child of a King. And it is on my left rib cage by my heart. This freedom defines every area of my life.

Spiritual freedom is something that once tasted can not be lived without. It is true communion with the God who loves you unconditionally – a type of love that you will never fully experience here on earth. But the problem is that too often we are living so far in bondage that this type of spiritual freedom is foreign and unknown. Since we have lived our lives in a foreign land so full of deceit and lies, this sweet life of truth and abundance can seem out of reach.

To give you a better of idea of the different life that I now live spiritually and how this has played out in pragmatic ways:

My life in bondage	My life of freedom
Dreaded mornings	Jump out of bed in anticipation for the day - sometimes wake up in the middle of the night so excited about the morning
Wasted time going in circles	Accomplishing my goals with intention, more doors of opportunity opening than I could ever plan for myself
My mind was preoccupied	Able to focus on the here and now
My family was a lower priority	Having a blast with my family
I dreaded opening the monthly bills	I no longer pay any attention to the bills

Regularly checking bank balances	Only look as a part of planning
Lacked exercise and motivation	Daily walks & power hours with a spring in my step
Rarely read any good books	Read for enjoyment, personal growth& pleasure
Praying was all about me	I love to pray for others
Dwelling on the past	Having vision and hope for the future
Longer hours and less $$	I spend less time working & earn significantly more

What sounds better? I realize that where you are at right now may make it almost seem impossible to see the other side. But remember where I came from – there's a good chance that I was deeper into bondage than where you are at right now. Part of the reason that I wrote this book was as a reminder – I never want to forget where I have come from and the lessons that I have learned.

Right now, today if you can't see your way out of the mess that you are in - remember that this will only strengthen your character if you will let it. And this will then prepare you for a very bright future:

> *"For I know the plans I have for you declares*
> *the Lord, plans to prosper you and not to harm*
> *you, plans to give you hope and a future."*
> The prophet Jeremiah

Is this not the life that you want to live? There is a loving God who wants to reveal the amazing future and plans that He has for your life. Or do you think that you have done a better job of it? Can you foresee things as clearly and accurately into the future as the one who created you and everything else around us? Wouldn't it be a nice change to know that everything is going to be better than great not just because of the 'power of positive thinking' or 'manifestations of the universe' but rather because your life is in the hands of your loving Heavenly Father? Don't dismiss this because of some negative experience that you once had with someone that called them self a Christian. To dismiss the love of God the Father and His son Jesus Christ because of how someone hurt you or misrepresented Him is a horrible idea. Nobody is perfect – the only perfect, sinless one to ever walk this earth was crucified. So to try and hold someone else to this level and be hurt or angry when they let us down is idiotic. Sorry – just calling it like it is.

The big blessing is to be able to live your life as you were designed to. Rather than living life trying to please others and trying to be who you think others want you to be, you become the person who your creator has created you to be. Once you get here, you will wake up in the mornings ready to be a blessing to others. And knowing that regardless of people's reactions and responses to you, you are free to be the special person that you were intricately designed to be. God knows every part of you so I encourage you to allow Him to do His work in you. He knows what you need.

"God, investigate my life; get all the facts firsthand. I'm an open book to you; even from a distance, you know what I'm thinking. You know when I leave and when I get back; I'm never out of your sight. You know everything I'm going to say before I start the first sentence. I look behind me and you're there, then up ahead and you're there, too— your reassuring presence, coming and going. This is too much, too wonderful— I can't take it all in! Is there anyplace I can go to avoid your Spirit? To be out of your sight? If I climb to the sky, you're there! If I go underground, you're there! If I flew on morning's wings to the far western horizon, You'd find me in a minute— you're already there waiting! Then I said to myself, "Oh, he even sees me in the dark! At night I'm immersed in the light!" It's a fact: darkness isn't dark to you; night and day, darkness and light, they're all the same to you. Oh yes, you shaped me first inside, then out; you formed me in my mother's womb. I thank you, High God—you're breathtaking! Body and soul, I am marvelously made! I worship in adoration—what a creation! You know me inside and out, you know every bone in my body; You know exactly how I was made, bit by bit, how I was sculpted from nothing into something. Like an open book, you watched me grow from conception to birth; all the stages of my life were spread out before you, The days of my life all prepared before I'd even lived one day. Your thoughts—how rare, how beautiful! God, I'll never comprehend them! I couldn't even begin to count them— any more than I could count the sand of the sea. Oh, let me rise in the morning and live always with you!

---Psalm 139

With the freedom that I have discovered and the truth that I have been learning I have slowly been able to unwind the mess that I have been entwined in for the last 40+ years. And now I am truly living the life that my Father has wanted not only for me but for each of you reading this book. My hope with this book is to encourage as many as possible and to be able to guide you on the way to where your loving God wants you to be. I hope that I was transparent enough to give you hope for a better future. Don't just shut this book, put it on the shelf and move on to another self help book to try and find life's answers. Consider my words, listen and learn from the mistakes that I have made and then talk to God. Ask him to reveal Himself to you so that things in your life will begin to make more sense. And then take time to listen. God wants us to be still and silent. If we don't take the time to do this, then hearing from Him is difficult.

If you have been challenged and are now breathing in freedom and for the first time are getting the oxygen you need in your soul then I suggest that you pass this book on to someone you care about who also needs to be free. I would also consider it an honor to hear your feedback, questions or chat further with you – please email me at freedom@FreedomPS.ca

Now that you have a picture of what freedom means to me and its importance in my life I have to make a final point extremely clear.

You will only ever have a small taste of freedom here on earth. In order to have your appetite for freedom completely satisfied you need to join me for eternity in heaven. I hope that you will consider this very carefully before you put my book on the shelf.

Action

Is God saying anything to you? Have you been ignoring Him as He has been calling you? I promise you that if you spend some time seeking him that you will find him. Take a minute to note what grabbed you in regards to experiencing some tremendous spiritual freedom.

<u>Post Game</u>

I.   <u>A snapshot of my financial health before and…</u>

I don't share this to get your sympathy or applause; it is to give you some hope that drastic change can happen when you have clear direction and a map of how to get there. I give God 100% of all the credit for getting me where I needed to go. He gave me the strength and perseverance when it would have been a lot easier to just throw in the towel. He opened the doors for me to enter when I was ready. As I am writing this, I am in the process of walking through some of these which I will share more with you later.

Below is the "rags" portion of my story. We are close to being able to share the remaining"riches"part. Stay tuned and join the **"Freedom Fighter Network"** at www.FreedomPS.ca to hear the rest of the story as it unfolds.

- We still owed $150k on a house that was foreclosed
- We had several maxed out credit cards and loans on things we no longer owned
- We had assets seized from our property
- Everyday I had to go to work because otherwise the family wouldn't eat next week. We were only a month away from being completely broke

- We had lost over $200,000 in investments and still had the leveraged debt
- We constantly had to track our bank balance to plan which minimum payment to make next and which bills to ignore.
- We learned how to ignore phone calls from unknown numbers because of the creditors and bill collectors that were harassing us
- I had lost my driver's license and had to manage my struggling business without being able to drive to meetings and appointments for 6 months.

II. My Day as P. Minister

1. Get the government out of any business that can be done better by the private sector. The government would still be involved in protecting the country's borders and dealing with criminals.

2. Transition the government out of the business of enabling helplessness with the CPP and EI programs. Educate people how to care for themselves and incentivize charities to fill this role.

3. Allow the economy to operate on its own without intervention; stop interfering. No BIG bank bailouts and currency manipulation. The banks exist to serve the public. Therefore change the laws that give the banks so much freedom; do not allow bail-ins either. Ensure that the people's money in the banks is safe.

4. Stop collaborating with the banksters and have the Bank of Canada operate as it was intended to do. Stop paying billions of $$ in interest payments to this group of fraudsters who operate the private banks. Convert the private debt of the country back into a public debt.

5. Shut down the CRA and discontinue income tax. Cover any deficit with a reasonable consumption tax – hoping that the GST is sufficient at 5% to do so.

6. Accumulate gold reserves and back our fiat currency so it is 'money' again. Be the leader in this so our currency becomes recognized on a global scale.

7. Make deficit spending against the law.

8. Get the country out of debt and enable new industries to emerge to attract the international markets so our exports can increase and our currency used more globally.

9. Educate citizens about the truth of freedom and enable people to be free. Show Canadians that we can live in the land of the free as our national anthem boasts and Bill of Rights proclaims.

10. Tear up the Canadian Charter of Rights and work with the Bill of Rights to become our true constitution.

Some of these things may meet a little bit of resistance and be somewhat idealistic but that's what you do when you are P. Minister for a day.

III.   Tangible Steps to Freedom

My goal with these parting thoughts is to give you some tangible steps that you can take in order to experience an amazing freedom. There are some areas of freedom that I am continuing to discover that I was hoping to have completely figured out before I published the book. I can share with you some concepts for you to consider below and more later to be shared in the **"Freedom Fighter Network"** at www.FreedomPS.ca

Financial Freedom

For years in my role as a financial advisor I helped people lower the debt payments through structuring their mortgages differently. I also helped clients get the proper life insurance to protect their families. The part that gave me the most satisfaction was moving money out of under performing assets in the stock market (mutual funds) into hard assets such as real estate, precious metals and colored investment grade diamonds.

But what I have enjoyed learning the most is the concept of converting debt into money. If you understand what I wrote about the fraud of the banksters, then you will love this.

After understanding the fraud behind debt; I understood the possibility of converting debt into money. It's not done through the court (legal) system. It's not done with the help of a lawyer. It's done using the universal law of the UCC

(Uniform Commercial Code). An organization that I have been following has spent the last 8 years putting together the infrastructure to make this all possible. I understood all the principles behind it but wasn't sure if they would be able to pull it off. The timing of publishing my book was supposed to be based on them launching the funding. I will continue to follow their progress and share updates as they occur. This may never come to fruition since it's a mammoth undertaking and history in the making. But if it does you will want to hear about it and be at the front of the line.

Stay Tuned!

Some Food For Thought

Is the food we eat really good for us or are we blindly lead to believe everything they sell in the stores has passed some kind of FDA approval to be safe for consumption?

GMO's, Yellow #5, Manufactured Glutamic Acid (the active ingredient in Monosodium Glutamate) or by many other names, textured soy protein concentrate, Carrageenan (E 407), Gelatin, hydrolyzed protein, Whey protein isolate, maltodextrin, Calcium caseinate, Sodium caseinate, modified cornstarch are all names used instead of MSG.

Also Aspartame, Tartrazine, Propylene glycol alginate (E405), Enriched Flour, Polysorbate 60, High Fructose Corn Syrup, Butylated Hydroxytoluene (BHT) a product also used in jet fuel and embalming fluid. A lot of these so called ingredients cause cancer, liver damage, contain mercury and metallic iron.

Check your food labels; you will find these ingredients everywhere, even in so called 'healthy food'. Can you believe these hidden ingredients were all passed by the FDA as to be safe for human consumption, then WHY do they have to hide them behind different names?

Gone are the days when farmers didn't have to inject their cows or chickens with any hormones to make them grow just to compete with other farmer's crops or livestock for selection. The animals ate off the land and the land provided. Why have things changed so drastically and for the worse? Is there something that we need to be aware of?

It is possible that digestive/bowel disorders will surpass cancer as the #1 killer. Our own food source is killing us from the inside out.

All these toxins and foreign ingredients are in our bodies from man-made chemicals and substances which we can't even pronounce. It's not good, but people keep eating it and buying it so they keep making it. Simple supply and demand formula says that they wouldn't make it if we didn't buy it!

So what do we do...read labels...don't eat anything if you can't pronounce or don't know what it is. Start taking the time to make your own food instead of trusting someone else to make it for you. Raise chickens, grain feed them; hunt for your own meat, use almond flour and coconut flour. Eat only what comes from the earth, meat, fruit and vegetables. Don't eat anything that comes in a box. Read, read and read some more; the more informed you are the better choices you will make for you and your family.

We have become lazy eaters and merely consumers instead of investigators; just because the FDA cleared a certain ingredient doesn't mean it's safe for consumption... remember it is a government agency controlling another area of our lives.

Since we do not want to depend on the commercial food industry we are planning to build our own Aquaponics system. This will be a symbiotic system where we will have fresh fish and vegetables that will be sustaining each other. You may have read about these systems; ours is using a patented technology from a local company that a good friend of mine is involved with. Can you imagine being able to grow a tomato from seed to being on your plate in 30 days? Or watching your greens growing 1 ½ inches per day? No pesticides. No fertilizers. No herbicides. Less water. And some fish for a little protein to top it off.

Stay tuned!

Something to Energize You

Chicken Fat is more than just finger lickin' good

In 2002 I purchased a VW Golf to test out biodiesel. I did a lot of research online to discover that I could fuel my car with lard. So I put a 45 gallon drum out back of KFC and asked them to throw all of their chicken fat into my drum. In 2 weeks I had collected 45 gallons of the liquid gold. With a little ethanol and lye I had created approximately 35 gallons of biofuel and 10 gallons of glyceride soap. For the next 6 months and 10,000 km I chugged along filling the highways with the sweet smell of a drumstick and it cost me only .17per litre.

It was difficult to get anyone too excited about using the KFC flavored soap so I added some lilac fragrance. I also liked the idea of it being an exfoliant so without too much research I decided to add crushed up some peanut shells. For one of my friends who loved what I did, I gave him and his wife some towels and soap as a gift for their wedding. A couple of weeks later I got a call thanking me for the large scrape across his chest – it was a little more exfoliation than he had bargained for!

I Love Free Energy

Nikola Tesla was a brilliant man whose inventions haven't impacted the world in the same way as Thomas Edison's...yet! Tesla's work was to help people have free energy and Edison's enabled BIG business and BIG banks to control this energy. In 1893 at the World Exposition in Chicago Tesla demonstrated his AC power free energy to the world. Nikola Tesla was on the verge of helping the world to access this free energy until JP Morgan caught wind of it. Realizing how this would negatively impact the bankster's control of the people, Tesla's financing ceased. And now 100 years later his concepts are just barely being made public. It's time to put Tesla's work to use and show the world that energy is more easily and readily available than what we have grown accustomed to over the last century. It is not necessary to have monopolies control the power grid and to have to pay for what is at all of our fingertips for free.

I am in the process of testing out how I can use Tesla's brilliance to power my home. I was hoping to have something already working before the book was published. I will get to this soon. The book has been taking too much of my time.

Stay tuned!

Something to Feed Your Soul

Our spiritual lives are the foundation of who we are. We have all been created with a spirit that is an empty vacuum until we fill it with the love of our God. Our lives will remain empty of the full potential that we were destined for and can't live it to the max without a relationship with God.

I don't like doing this kind of thing in a book because it can come across as being religious and in a step by step fashion that doesn't get across what Jesus wants us to hear. Jesus put it very simply so I will too; that if you confess with your mouth that Jesus is Lord and believe in your heart that He was raised from the dead that you will be saved. If this is something that you want to further explore please send me an email. I would love to get you started on what will be the most important and exciting journey that you have ever been on.

It has been a pleasure to spend the last few hours together.

I hope that you have gotten a sense of the love for freedom that I have. Because I have lived in both extremes (freedom and bondage) and have seen so many others on the bondage side, I have an intense passion to lead as many of you to this world of freedom that is so incredible. You need to decide if you would rather live a life of regrets like George did or end the madness and begin your life of freedom and abundance today. As my forerunner and awesome Scottish mentor William Wallace so eloquently declares:

"FRRRREEEEEEEEDDOOOOOMMMMMM!!!!!"

P.S. There are several aspects of freedom that I am still discovering. I have held off publishing this book for several months hoping that I would be ready to go deeper into some of these areas. I have decided to publish and will have ongoing updates as the freedom journey progresses. I will share with you examples of what has worked on my road to financial freedom and beyond. If you are interested in staying in touch, then I invite you to join

"The Freedom Fighter Network"

Doug's Top ~~10~~ 11 Reasons why you want to join the FFN:

1. Top buy rate for junk gold jewelry offered.
2. Learn how to provide vegetables and fish year round using the best ever acquaponics system.
3. Receive top strategies of how to protect your assets and keep as much of your $$ as possible.
4. Learn how to invest in the same assets as the ultra wealthy – special elite offers to members.
5. Hear encouraging stories from those who have experienced a 180 and found freedom and build community with these freedom fighters.
6. Be a part of my journey to testing free energy and other solutions to corporate bondage.
7. Have an opportunity to receive financial coaching. I will be offering some individual consulting to a few each month.
8. Monthly webinars that will keep members up to date with opportunities and tips.
9. Receive help and suggestions to find freedom in your relationships and overall health.
10. Receive special offers for discounts and deals on everyday items. (The world's largest loyalty program)
11. There will be a monthly silver give-a-way!!! 1 oz of **Liberty** to a lucky winner each month

Go now to www.FreedomPS.ca

God bless you on your journey.

Douglas G. Loewen

freedom@FreedomPS.ca

www.FreedomPS.ca/youtube

www.FreedomPS.ca/facebook

www.FreedomPS.ca/twitter

.

22223810R00066

Made in the USA
Charleston, SC
12 September 2013